the MEDIEVAL CASTLE

A. G. Smith

DOVER PUBLICATIONS, INC.
MINEOLA, NEW YORK

Bibliographical Note

The Medieval Castle is a new work, first published by Dover Publications, Inc., in 2002.

International Standard Book Number

ISBN-13: 978-0-486-42080-6
ISBN-10: 0-486-42080-9

Manufactured in the United States by Courier Corporation
42080905   2014
www.doverpublications.com

NOTE

In the turbulent times of the Middle Ages, when strong national governments did not yet exist, and kings and lords, knights and nobles, natives and invaders vied for power and property all across Europe, a strong castle represented some measure of safety and security for its owner, as well as for serfs, servants and nearby townspeople. In addition to its role as a defensive fortress, the castle also served as a residence for the local lord and his family.

Early medieval castles were of the motte-and-bailey type, consisting of a fortified building (keep) of stone or wood atop a motte (mound), surrounded by a ward or bailey (open area), the whole encircled by a ditch. The baileys, at the foot of the mound, were enclosed by palisades and later by walls and towers of masonry. Later castles were almost all built of stone, since wood had two major drawbacks: it eventually decayed and it was very vulnerable to fire. Gradually, castles became larger, stronger, and more elaborate, as builders tried to eliminate weak points and make the castle as invulnerable as possible.

Although we often think of castles as places of warfare, in times of peace these great strongholds were simply the home of the resident king or lord and his family. Within the castle walls there was a kitchen, gardens, stables, a chapel for religious services, and a Great Hall, where meals were served and feasts took place, accompanied by such entertainment as music, acrobatics, and juggling. There was also a keep or donjon, which served as the living quarters for the resident family. Strongly built and heavily fortified, the keep was also the last place of refuge for the occupants if invading forces succeeded in forcing their way into the castle. In addition, many castles featured a postern, a smaller gate or passage that could be used to escape from the castle if all hope was lost.

Large stone castles were exceedingly difficult to conquer, but invading armies had many military tricks up their sleeves. Catapults were used to throw stones and other missiles—even dead animals (to spread disease)—over the walls. Miners called "sappers" were trained to undermine a castle wall so that the wall eventually collapsed, allowing the besieging soldiers to enter. Siege towers could be rolled into place against the castle walls, enabling soldiers to clamber over the top. And if all else failed, the besieging army could try to starve the occupants out, cutting off delivery of food and other supplies until the inhabitants could hold out no longer.

Castle defenders, on the other hand, had their own means and methods of repelling a siege attack. The drawbridge over the moat was raised and a heavy gate called a portcullis lowered at the gatehouse entrance. Archers fired arrows from atop the castle walls, or through small openings in the walls called loops. Defenders dropped large stones and poured boiling water, pitch, and other substances down on the attackers. Sometimes they were able to set fire to the siege vehicles. In some cases, the invaders succeeded in gaining entry and taking the castle, but at other times the castle defenses were too strong, and the siege was lifted.

Although castles were impressive to look at and served their purpose as defensive fortresses well, they were probably not very comfortable places to live. Stone buildings, although strong and durable, tend to be dark, cold, and damp. In the Middle Ages, the only heat in the castle came from fireplaces, and some parts of the castle weren't heated at all. Tapestries and rugs were hung on the walls and over doorways to keep out draughts. The floors were strewn with rushes, and sometimes, herbs, but beneath the rushes, many castles had a layer of grease, spilled beer, animal bones, and other waste matter that must have been a source of unpleasant odors and, possibly, disease. Bathrooms were nothing more than a hole in a stone bench built into a projection of the castle wall, and although the nobility sometimes bathed (in large wooden tubs), serfs and commoners generally did not.

By the fifteenth century, when cannons and gunpowder revolutionized warfare, castles had reached the end of their usefulness as defensive fortresses. Cannons could easily reduce even the strongest castle walls to rubble, making these great strongholds obsolete. Today, their ruins still dot the European landscape, mute testimony to an era when castles symbolized safety and refuge in uncertain times, as well as the power and prestige of the king or local lord, and the rigid hierarchy of the feudal system.

During medieval times, mainly from the 1100s to the 1500s, large stone castles were built throughout Europe. These huge structures helped consolidate the king or lord's power over the land. The castle served as both a defensive fortress and as the residence of the local lord. Castles were usually the center of community life, and fairs were held in or near the castle on a regular basis.

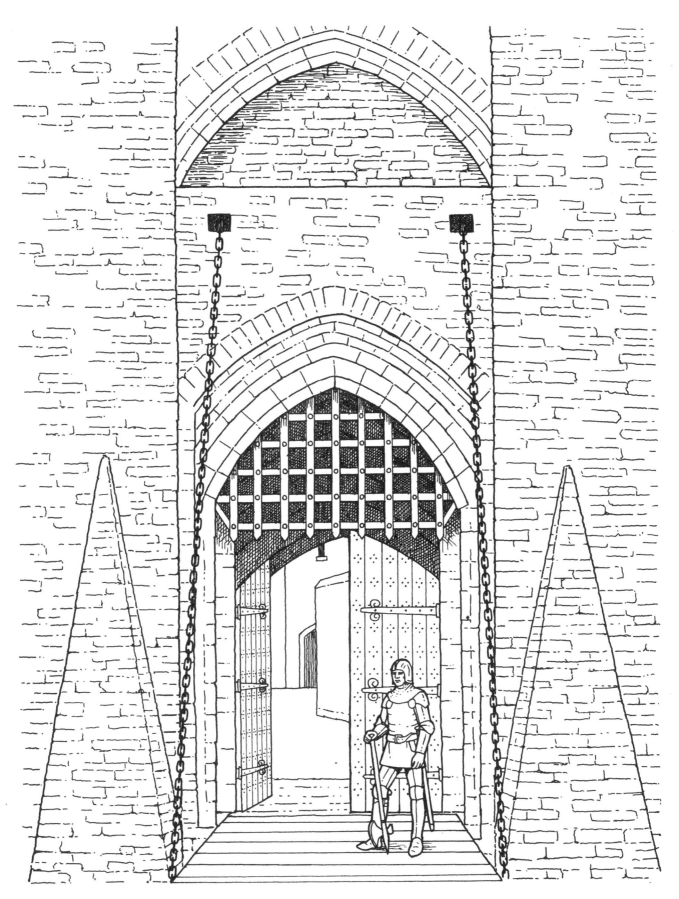

Entrance to the castle was by means of a gate-house, which was often part of a large tower called a barbican. Visitors had to cross a draw-bridge over a water-filled moat. The drawbridge could be raised or lowered, as could the portcullis, a heavy iron gate designed to allow entrance or to keep invaders out.

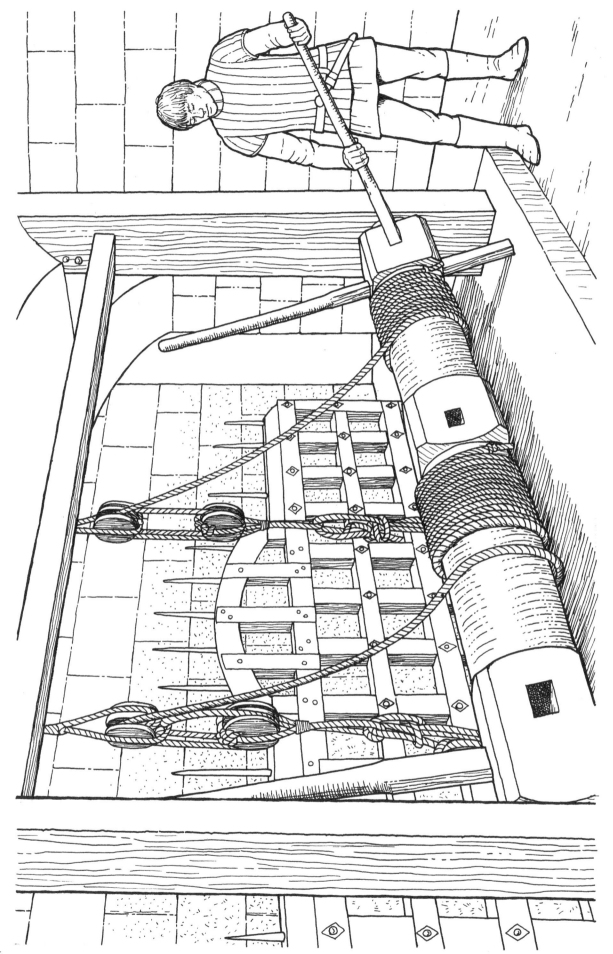

The portcullis was raised and lowered by a system of winches and ropes or chains housed in a room above the gatehouse.

6

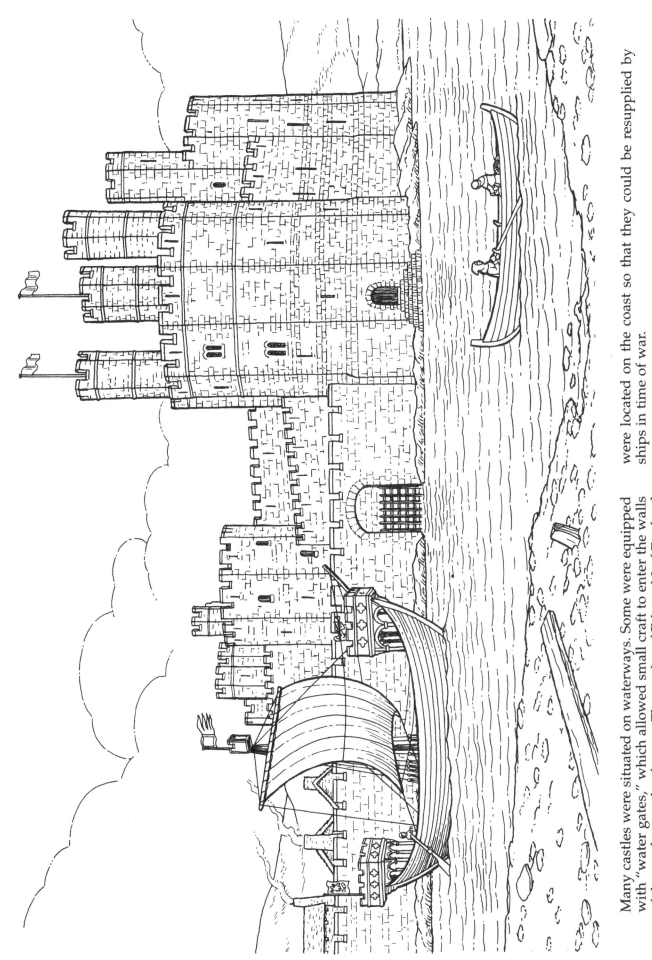

Many castles were situated on waterways. Some were equipped with "water gates," which allowed small craft to enter the walls of the castle to unload cargo. The castles of Edward I of England were located on the coast so that they could be resupplied by ships in time of war.

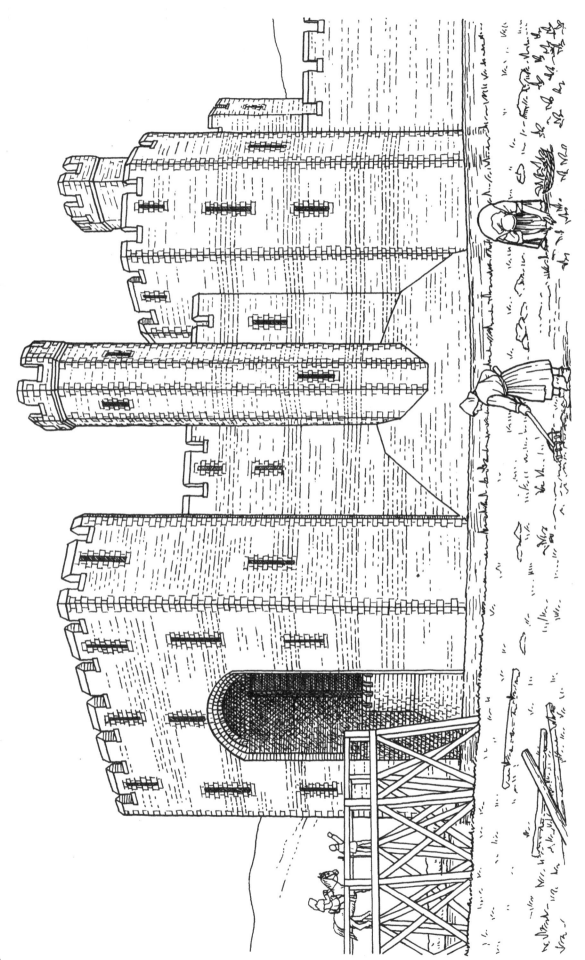

The castle above is entered by means of a wooden bridge. At the base of the turret to the right of the main gate, stonework called "battering" encircles the bottom of the tower. Battering was designed to prevent "sappers" (soldiers who specialized in undermining foundations) or battering rams from destroying the tower.

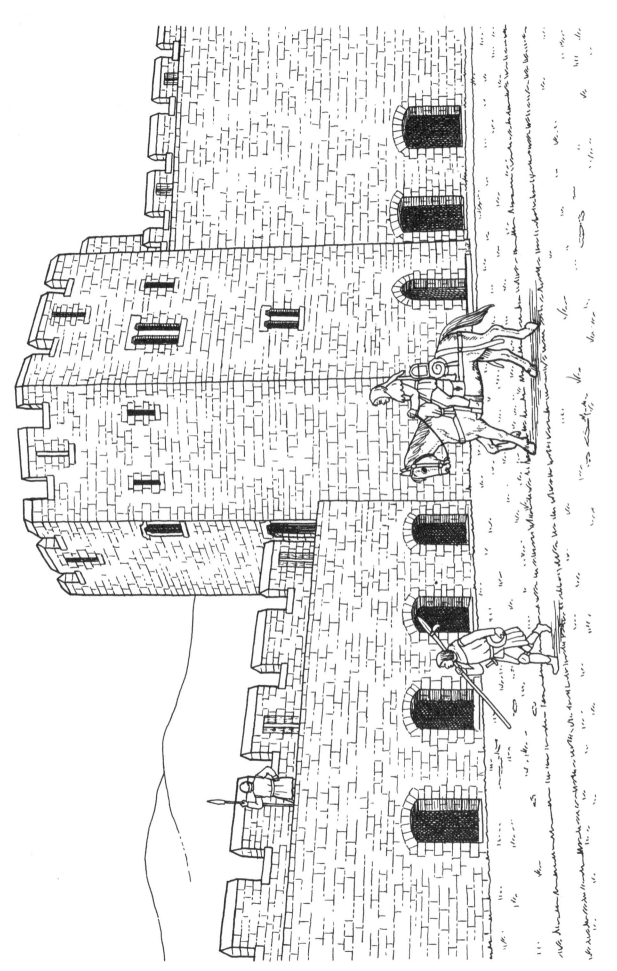

An interior view showing the "curtain" wall that enclosed the castle, and a tower. Castles sometimes had two curtain walls—an inner and an outer—designed to protect the castle against invaders. If the outer curtain was breached, the inner wall would still provide an obstacle to attackers. Curtain walls averaged thirty feet in height and were up to twenty feet thick.

A crossbowman stands guard in the interior of a curtain wall. Arrow slits in the wall allowed the bowman to fire his weapon without exposing himself to enemy fire.

A guard stands watch outside a fortified door. The most secure rooms in the castle—dungeons, the treasury, the wine cellar—were protected by heavy wooden doors bound in iron.

The Great Hall was the center of court life in the castle. Located in the bailey (the open courtyard within the castle walls), it was usually a large one-room structure with a great fireplace. At mealtimes, the lord and lady of the castle sat at a table on a raised dais. Feasts, usually with entertainment, took place in the Great Hall. It was also here that the king, or lord of the manor, received his vassals.

Exterior view of the Great Hall. Early halls were often built of timber, while later halls were built of stone, with plenty of windows to admit light. Glass was an expensive and highly prized commodity in the Middle Ages, so that many castles of earlier times used thin sheets of animal horn as window coverings. However, by the thirteenth century, the king and the greatest lords enjoyed windows of "white glass" (actually greenish) in the hall. By the fourteenth century, most halls boasted glazed windows.

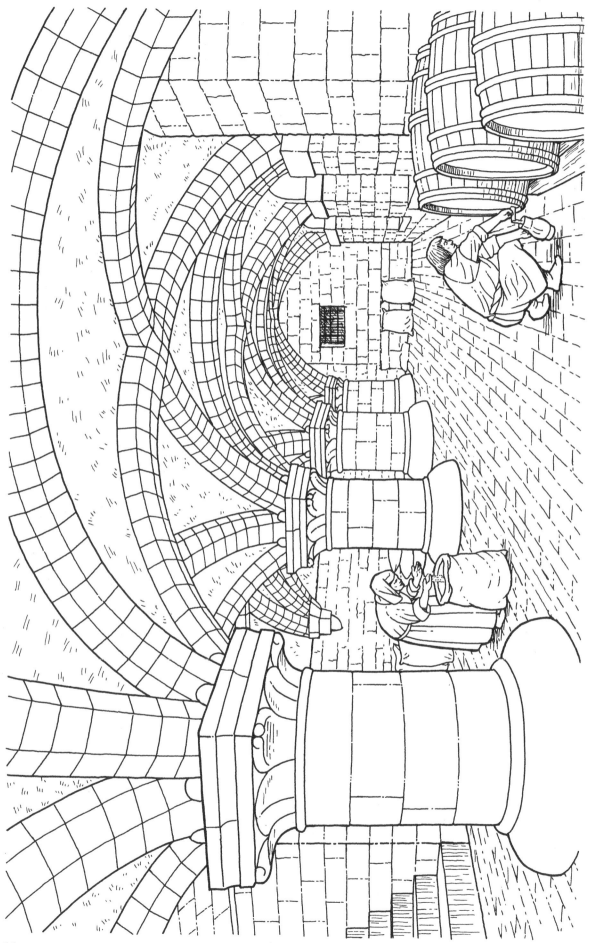

Wine, grain, cheese, beans, bread, rice, and other foods were often stored in the cellar beneath the Great Hall. Sometimes they were stored in the keep, where they could be kept under lock and key. Because there was no way to refrigerate or can foods, long-term storage of food was a problem. Large amounts of salt were used to help preserve meat after butchering, while abundant spices helped disguise the taste of food that had spoiled.

Early castle kitchens were made of wood and placed in a corner of the bailey. However, this necessitated a long trip to the Great Hall, by which time the food was often cold. Later kitchens were built of stone inside the Great Hall.

Some kitchens had huge ovens, capable of roasting two or three oxen at a time. This kitchen features a large central hearth where meats and other foods are stewed in a cauldron.

15

Often, many less important structures (such as the stables shown here) were built against the curtain wall, using towers or other masonry structures as the sides. In this picture, a farrier shoes a horse, while a groom tends to the others. Sometimes, when a castle under siege was running out of provisions, horses were killed for food.

Cross-section of the keep, or great tower. The keep was the most heavily fortified of the castle towers, with walls ten to twelve feet thick. Often divided into three or four stories, it was designed to sustain a long siege, and contained living and service quarters, storerooms and its own well. In some castles, dungeons were built in the bottom of the keep.

Parapet

Wall Walk

Turret

Gatehouse

Battering

Moat

Town Wall

Curtain Wall

Barbican and Gatehouse

Bird's eye view of a castle. As the town has grown around the castle, a wall has been extended to surround the town. In times of danger, the townspeople would seek refuge in the castle. Some of

18

Great Hall

Keep or Donjon

Bailey or Ward

Wall Tower

Arrow Loop

Drawbridge

Gateway

the town houses have thatched roofs, making them extremely vulnerable to fire. The roofs of the buildings within the castle are covered with slates, shingles, or sheets of lead.

Interior of a tower room with a hooded fireplace. In early castles, heat was provided by a central hearth, however, these were inconvenient and a fire hazard. Fireplaces, built into the wall, eventually replaced central hearths. The fireplace generated heat both directly and by radiation from the stones at the back. A projecting hood of stone or plaster helped funnel the smoke up the chimney.

The chapel was the spiritual center of the castle. It was usually located close to the living quarters of the lord and his family, who attended mass each morning. Pious knights prayed in the chapel before a battle or prior to embarking on a crusade.

A lady of the castle tends to her needlework, while seated in a window seat set into the thick tower wall. Since windows represented easy entry points for intruders, they were generally not found below the second or third floors. In later times, castles featured the oriel, a kind of cozy nook, with windows and even a fireplace.

The castle under siege. The moat has been filled with logs and earth to enable the attackers to roll a movable siege tower close to the castle wall. From the top of the tower, the enemy has lowered a ramp over the top of the wall and hoardings (timber galleries projecting out from the battlements, with openings in their floors that allowed castle defenders to drop stones or other missiles on the enemy below), and is attempting to gain access to the castle.

Catapults were able to cast stones or flaming balls of pitch over the castle walls. It is even said that catapults were used to throw the heads of slain enemies into the castle, instilling fear and hor- ror in the occupants. A catapult was smaller and less powerful than a similar weapon called the trebuchet.

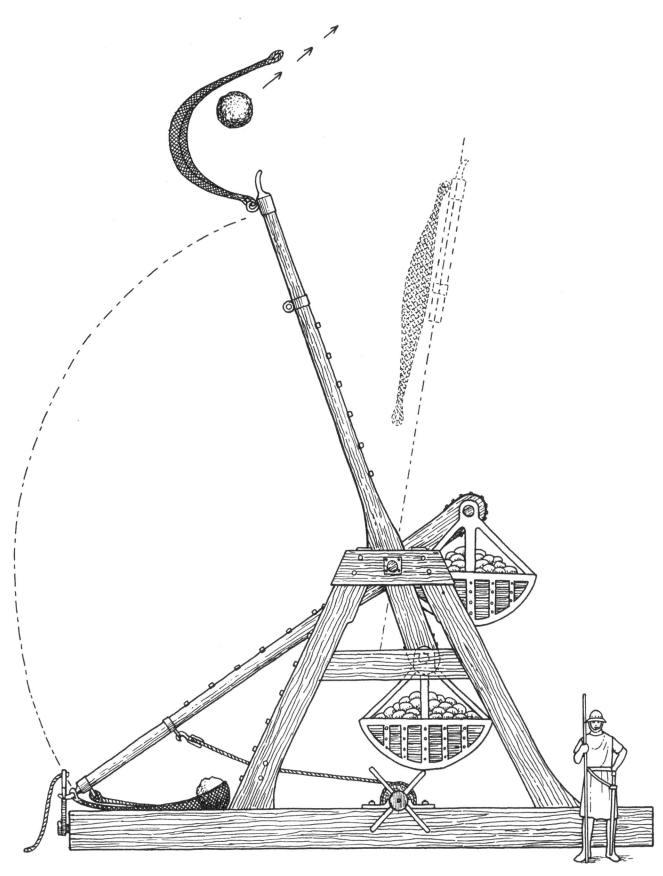

The trebuchet was a large siege engine capable of throwing huge stones (up to 400 lbs.) and other missiles. More accurate than the catapult, the trebuchet could pound away at a particular spot in the castle wall until the wall crumbled. Early versions were powered by human muscle, but later models employed a large counterweight to propel the arm forward, launching a missile from the sling at the end of the arm.

Drill

Battering Ram

Cannon

Other siege weapons: 1. A huge drill, used to pry apart the seams of the castle walls. 2. The bosson, or battering ram, which was brought close to a gate, and continually rammed against it until the gate gave way. 3. The cannon. The introduction of cannons and gunpowder c. 1400, and their ability to reduce castle walls to rubble, spelled the end of the stone castle as a defensive fortress.

The castle wall being attacked under cover of a penthouse or "cat," a long one-story structure built of stout timbers and covered with raw hides (the hides were kept wet to prevent them from being set afire). Miners or sappers would dig out a large chamber underneath the castle wall, propping up the wall with timbers. They then set the timber alight. When the props burned away, the wall would collapse into the chamber, allowing the invaders to enter through the breach. In this picture, a stone flung from a catapult has destroyed a section of the timber hoardings atop the castle wall.

Gateways and passageways giving entrance to the castle often featured "murder holes" in the ceiling and side walls, through which defenders dropped stones, and other missiles, and shot arrows at the attacking forces.

Spiral staircases within the thick tower walls were constructed from interlocking steps. They were usually designed to allow those defending them from above the greatest room to swing their swords, while giving less room to the attacker coming up the steps.

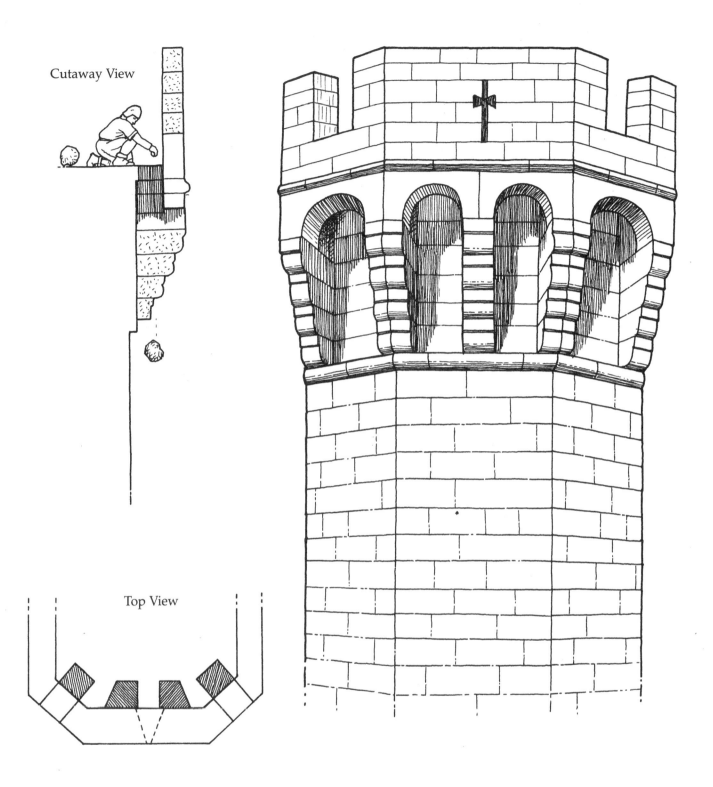

Cutaway View

Top View

A machicolated tower. Machicolations were openings formed in the roofs of gateways and entrance passages through which defenders, protected by stone walls, could hurl stones, boiling pitch, darts and other missiles on the assailants below. In later castles, stone machicolations replaced the temporary wooden hoardings of earlier times.

30

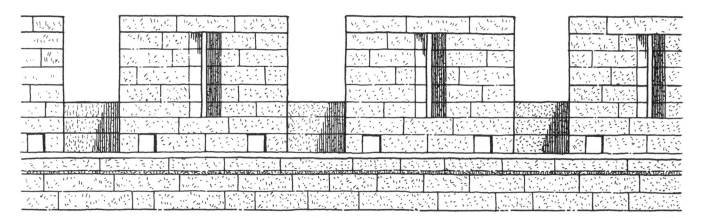

Inside View

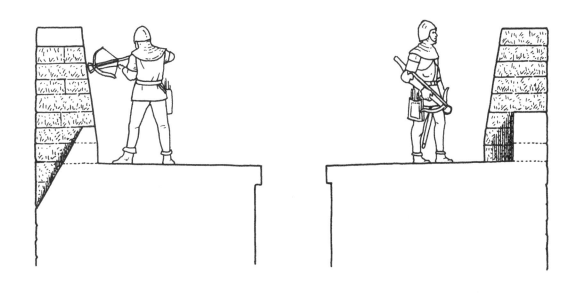

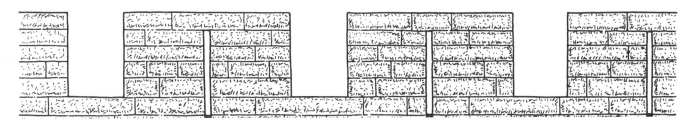

Outside View

Interior and exterior views of castle wall sections showing arrow slits, and put-log holes in which timbers were inserted for building scaffolding and for extending wooden hoardings.

A crossbowman on the wall walk keeps a sharp eye out for approaching enemies, while a long-bowman mounts the steps. The crossbow was a formidable weapon, with far greater power and range than the longbow. However, it was slow and inconvenient to load. A trained longbowman could get off four or five shots to the crossbowman's one.